PONTYPOOL TO MOUNTAIN ASH

Vic Mitchell and Keith Smith

MP **Middleton Press**

EVOLVING THE ULTIMATE RAIL ENCYCLOPEDIA

Cover picture: From the unhurried 1950s: the guard stands at ease while the photographer records 0-6-2T no. 5679 at Hengoed High Level with a Pontypool Road to Neath service. (M.J.Stretton coll.)

Published September 2005

ISBN 1 904474 65 9

© Middleton Press, 2005

Design Deborah Esher

Published by
          Middleton Press
          Easebourne Lane
          Midhurst, West Sussex
          GU29 9AZ
Tel: 01730 813169
Fax: 01730 812601
Email: info@middletonpress.co.uk
www.middletonpress.co.uk

Printed & bound by Biddles Ltd, Kings Lynn

INDEX

ACKNOWLEDGEMENTS

We are very grateful for the assistance received from many of those mentioned in the credits also to A.R.Carder, R.Caston, L.Crosier, G.Croughton, E.A.Evans, D.K.Jones, B.J.King, N.Langridge, B.Lewis, Mr D. and Dr S.Salter, N.W.Sprinks and particularly our ever supportive wives, Barbara Mitchell and Janet Smith.

I.   The route map first appeared in the Railway Magazine in 1956 and the dashes indicate the lines closed by that time. The key to the figures near the margins is below and shows the early operating companies and the years in use; sometimes freight continued after loss of passenger service. The abbreviations are explained in the text that follows.

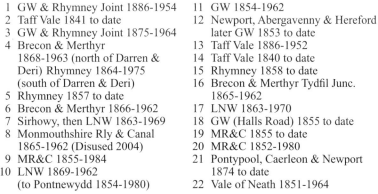

1	GW & Rhymney Joint 1886-1954	11	GW 1854-1962
2	Taff Vale 1841 to date	12	Newport, Abergavenny & Hereford
3	GW & Rhymney Joint 1875-1964		later GW 1853 to date
4	Brecon & Merthyr	13	Taff Vale 1886-1952
	1868-1963 (north of Darren &	14	Taff Vale 1840 to date
	Deri) Rhymney 1864-1975	15	Rhymney 1858 to date
	(south of Darren & Deri)	16	Brecon & Merthyr Tydfil Junc.
5	Rhymney 1857 to date		1865-1962
6	Brecon & Merthyr 1866-1962	17	LNW 1863-1970
7	Sirhowy, then LNW 1863-1969	18	GW (Halls Road) 1855 to date
8	Monmouthshire Rly & Canal	19	MR&C 1855 to date
	1865-1962 (Disused 2004)	20	MR&C 1852-1980
9	MR&C 1855-1984	21	Pontypool, Caerleon & Newport
10	LNW 1869-1962		1874 to date
	(to Pontnewydd 1854-1980)	22	Vale of Neath 1851-1964

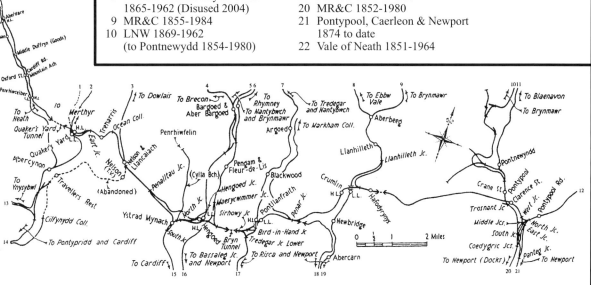

GEOGRAPHICAL SETTING

The maps are scaled at 15ins to 1 mile and north is at the top, unless otherwise stated.

From Pontypool the route climbed steeply out of the valley of the Avon Llwyd, more than two miles being at 1 in 45. It passed through the narrow limestone ridge surrounding the coalfield to enter the deep Ebbw Vale, which it traversed on the lofty Crumlin Viaduct.

A steady descent following to Pontllanfraith, where the Sirhowy Valley was crossed. Bryn Tunnel was built to provide gentle gradients to the Rhymney Valley, which was passed over on Hengoed Viaduct. This also marked the boundary between England and Wales, in the days before Monmouthshire was part of the latter.

The route passed over further high ground before reaching the deep Cwm Bargoed at Treharris. It soon entered the Taff Vale and crossed it at Quakers Yard. A further tunnel was required to allow the line to descend into the valley of the Avon Cynon, near Penrhiwceiber. It continued past the last of many collieries to reach Mountain Ash. The Welsh section was in the county of Glamorganshire.

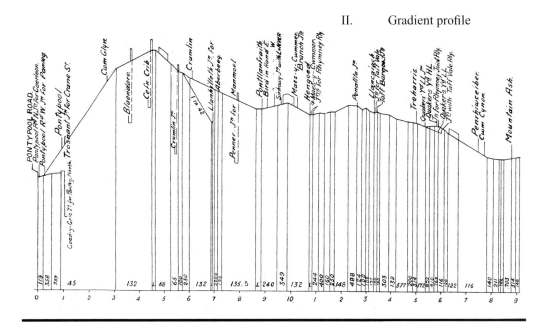

II.　　　Gradient profile

HISTORICAL BACKGROUND

The Newport, Abergavenny & Hereford Railway's other main route was aimed at Merthyr and it was opened from Pontypool to Crumlin on 20th August 1855. It was extended to Pontllanfraith on 15th October 1857, to Quakers Yard on 11th January 1858 and this was known as the Taff Vale Extension.

The NAHR became part of the West Midland Railway in June 1860, which in turn was absorbed by the Great Western Railway on 1st August 1863.

In the meantime, the Vale of Neath Railway had reached Aberdare on 24th September 1851 (it became part of the GWR in 1865). The line was extended east to the Aberdare Canal in 1856 by the Aberdare Valley Railway and this was controlled by the VofNR from 1864.

It fell to the GWR to close the gap and the

section through Mountain Ash and Middle Duffryn was opened on 5th October 1864, this allowing through running between Hereford and Swansea. However, most of the traffic ran over only short lengths of the route and was mainly mineral, notably coal.

The VofNR and some tracks east of Aberdare were of broad gauge initially and of mixed gauge from 1863 until 1872, standard gauge prevailing thereafter in South Wales.

The GWR became the Western Region of British Railways upon nationalisation in 1948. Passenger service between Pontypool Road and Neath via Mountain Ash was withdrawn on 11th June 1964. Through freight service between Pontypool and Aberdare was withdrawn on 15th June 1964, although some local freight use continued. This is detailed in the captions.

PASSENGER SERVICES

The initial service to Crumlin was three trains daily and this continued upon extension to Pontllanfraith (Tredegar Junction) in 1857. Further extension to Quakers Yard in 1858 brought an additional train daily; some ran through to Merthyr, usually two.

Following completion of the Middle Duffryn link in 1865, the GWR provided three through trains daily between Hereford and Swansea, but the Merthyr service was withdrawn. A similar frequency was maintained over the route covered by this album for most of the 19th century, although there were only two Sunday trains for most of that period; there were few after World War I on Sundays.

For most of the 20th century, there were five to seven trains between Pontypool Road and Neath with two of them continuing to Swansea in the early years.

In the 1940s, there was an additional train between Pontypool Road and Aberdare, plus one between Ystrad Mynach and Neath. There were also some local trains for workmen over sections of the route in later decades.

June 1922

PONTYPOOL ROAD, ABERDARE, MERTHYR, NEATH, and SWANSEA.—Great Western.

Week Days only.

Miles fm Pon. Rd.	Down.	mrn	mrn	mrn	mrn	mrn	mrn	mrn	mrn	mrn	aft	mrn	mrn	aft	aft	mrn	aft	aft	aft	aft	aft	aft
	102 London (Pad.) ....dep.	....	....	....	....	1 A 0	....	....	....	5 30	....	8 45	9 0	....	....	1150	....	1 10	....	3 35	....	....
	Pontypool Road ....dep.	6 35	....	....	....	7 45	8 47	....	....	11 2	....	1 24	2 20	....	....	4 55	....	6 15	....	7 25	....	....
1¼	Pontypool * **74, 75**	6 41	....	....	....	7 51	8 53	....	....	11 8	....	1 32	2 26	....	....	5 1	....	6 22	....	7 31	....	....
5¼	Hafodyrynys Platform	6 51	....	....	....	8 1	9 7	....	....	1118	....	1 42	2 36	....	....	5 11	....	6 32	....	7 41	....	....
6¾	Crumlin (High Level) † **93** ..	6 58	....	....	....	8 7	9 13	....	....	1123	....	1 49	2 43	....	....	5 17	....	6 39	....	7 49		....
9	Pontllanfraith **504**	7 4	....	....	....	8 13	9 20	....	....	1130	....	1 56	2 49	....	....	5 23	....	6 47	....	7 56		....
11	Hengoed & Maesycwmmer	7 10	....	....	....	8 20	9 30	....	....	1139	....	2 4	2 59	....	....	5 31	....	6 58	....	8 6		....
14	Nelson & Llancaiach 109, 111 arr.	Stop	....	....	....	8 26	9 37	....	....	1145	....	2 10	3 5	....	....	5 37	....	7 5	....	8 12	Saturdays only.	....
	dep.		....	....	....	8 27	9 39	....	....	1146	....	2 12	3 6	....	....	5 38	....	7 13	....	8 13		....
15¼	Treharris	....	....	....	....	8 31	9 44	....	....	1151	....	2 16	3 10	....	....	5 42	....	7 19	....	8 17		....
16	Quakers Yard (H. L.) 111, 115 arr.	....	....	....	....	8 34	9 47	....	....	1154	....	2 19	3 13	....	....	5 45	....	7 22	....	8 20		....
	dep.	....	....	....	....	8 36	9 52	....	....	1157	....	2 22	3 16	....	....	5 48	....	7 25	....	8 23		....
17¾	Penrhiwceiber **115**	....	....	....	....	8 41	9 57	....	....	12 2	....	2 27	3 21	....	....	5 53	....	7 30	....	8 28		....
19	Mountain Ash	....	....	m	....	8 46	10 5	m	....	12 7	m	2 32	3 28	....	m	5 53	....	7 36	m	8 34		....
21¼	Cwmbach Halt	mrn	....	8 5	....	....	....	1125		....	1 15	....	....		5 5	....			8 10	....	m	....
22¾	**Aberdare** ¶	7 30	....	8 12	....	8 58	1021	1129	....	1220	1 22	2 40	3 45	....	5 10	6 11	....	7 44	8 14	8 50	9 0	....
26¼	Hirwain ¶ (*below*) ....arr.	7 38	....	8 22	....	9 7	1033	....	....	1228	1 32	Stop	3 54	....	5 20	6 19	....	Stop	....	9 0	9 14	....
—	Mls. **Merthyr** ....dep.	7 10	....	....	....	8 40	10 5	....	....	1155	1 5		3 25		....	5 50	....		....	8 30	....	....
—	3¾ Abernant	7 20	....	....	....	8 50	1016	....	....	12 6	1 15	....	3 36	....	....	6 1	....		....	8 41	....	....
—	5½ Llwydcoed	7 24	....	....	....	8 54	1020	....	....	1210	1 20	....	3 40	....	....	6 5	....		....	8 45	....	....
—	7½ Hirwain (*below*) ...arr.	7 30	....	....	....	9 0	1026	....	....	1216	1 26	....	3 46	....	....	6 11	....		....	8 51	....	....
—	Hirwain ¶ ....dep.	7 44	....	8 24	m	9 10	1038	....		1235	1 33	aft	4 0	....	5 21	6 23	....	....	....	9 7	9 15	m
32¾	Glyn Neath	7 57	....	8 43	9 0	9 23	1052	....	m	1248	1 50	m	4 14	....	5 39	6 36	m	....	....	9 21	9 32	10 10
35¾	Resolven ¶	8 6	....	8 52	9 7	9 30	11 1	....	1145	1255	1 59	3 25	4 22	....	5 49	6 42	6 55	....	....	9 29	....	10 17
40	Aberdylais	8 15	....	9 5	9 20	9 39	1110	....	12 0	1 4	2 12	3 40	4 31	....	6 2	6 51	7 10	....	....	9 38	....	10 30
—	**Neath** (Low Level)	....	....	9 10	9 24	....	....	....	12 5	....	2 18	3 45	....	....	6 10	....	7 14	....	....	....	....	....
42¾	Neath Abbey ¶		....	9 14	....	....	....	....	12 9	....	2 22	3 49	....	....	6 14	....	....	....	....	....	....	....
45½	Briton Ferry Road		....	9 21	....	....	....	....	1216	....	2 29	3 56	....	....	6 21	....	....	....	....	....	....	....
48½	**Swansea** (East Dock) arr.	....	....	9 27	....	....	....	....	1222	....	2 35	4 2	....	....	6 27	....	....	aft	....	....	....	....
41¾	**Neath** (Town) **65, 689** ...	s 20	8 31	....	....	9 50	1122	....	....	1 18	....	....	4 43	5 1	....	7 0	....	7 7	....	9 51	....	10 35
43¾	Skewen	....	....	....	....	9 58	1129	....	....	1 26	....	....	....	5 8	....	....	....	7 14	....	9 58	....	....
46	Llansamlet	....	....	....	....	10 5	1136	....	....	1 33	....	....	....	5 14	....	....	....	7 20	....	10 5	....	....
48¾	Landore **60, 74**	....	8 45	....	....	1010	1141	....	....	1 40	....	....	....	5 19	....	....	....	7 25	....	10 10	....	....
49½	**Swansea** (High St.) **456** arr.	....	9 5	....	....	1020	1150	....	....	1 50	....	....	5 0	5 30	....	7 20	....	7 35	....	10 20	....	....

A Leaves London (Paddington) at 9 15 aft. on Sundays. m Motor Car, one class only. s Saturdays only.
* Clarence Street Station, about ½ mile to Crane Street Station. † About ¼ mile to Low Level Station.
"**Halts**" at Trecynon, between Aberdare and Hirwain; Rhigos and Pontwalby, between Hirwain and Glyn Neath; Melyncourt and Clyne, between Resolven and Aberdylais; and Cardonnel, between Neath Abbey and Briton Ferry Road.

PONTYPOOL ROAD, CARDIFF, MERTHYR, NEATH, and SWANSEA.

Week Days.

Down.																							
123 London (Pad.) ..... dep.				12 55								5 30		8 55	8 55		9 15		9 15			1155	1155
123 Bristol (Tem. M.) ,,				5 50	m		7 38				9 43		m	1110	11 10		1225		1 28		2 36	2 36
123 Newport (High St.) ,,		m		7 16	7 57	7 57	8 44	8 18	9 50		9 50		1040	1141	12 27		1252		1 28			2 36
Pontypool Road ..... dep.		6 40		7 42	8 25		8 42	9 45	1012		10 55		1143	1225	1 0		1 28		2 24		3 12	3 45
Pontypool **A** 78		6 45		7 47	8 29		8 47	9 49	1016		11 1		1147	1230	1 4		1 35		2 29		3 16	3 51
Hafodyrynys Platform [83	5 40	6 55		7 57		m	9 0	m	m		11 11			1240		m	1 46	m	2 39		m	4 1
Crumlin (H. Level) ¶ **B** 81	6 37	0		8 2	Stop	8 ?9	m	m			11 17			1245	1 12		1 52	2 48		4 7	4 37
Pentwynmawr Platform ..	6 07	6		8 6		8 439	11				11 17			1250	Stop		1 55	2	9		4 11	4 44
Penmaen Halt	6 13															2 14						4 49
Oakdale Halt ..... arr.	6 23															2 23						4 55
Pontllanfraith **C** 505		7 9		8 9	8 46	9 14					11 25			1253		1 58		2 51		m		Stop
Hengoed (High Level) **D**		7 14		8]20	8 50	9 20					11 33			1256		2 3		3 X 3				4 32
Nelson & Llancaiach 129 ar.		7 21		8 27		9 27				m	11 40				m	2 3		3 10		m		4 39
Mls Cardiff (Queen St.) ¶ dp.	Stop		6 33		8 20		9 10			1010	1050	12 0					1850		3 8		3 38
— 3¼ Llanishen ¶			6 45		7 57		9 22			1022	11 2	1212					2 2		3 20		3 49
— 7 Caerphilly			6 57		8 10		9 32			1031	1112	1223					2 15		3 31		4 1
— 9¼ Llanbradach			7 4	m	8 17		9 39			1040	1119	m					2 23		3 38		4 8
— 12¼ Ystrad Mynach .. [129			7 12	7 20	8 37		9 47			1047	1126	1237			1240		2 29		3 45		4 15
— 14½ Nelson & Llancaiach ar.				7 26	8 42		9 52			1052		1221			1246		3 52				
23¾ 24 .129 Dowlais **H** ..... arr.							1037				1 82			1 S3			3 47				
Nelson & Llancaiach ..... dep.			7 27	8 23	Stop		9 29		9 56		1053	11 47	1222			1247	2 11		3 11	3 55		4 40
15¾ Treharris ..... [92			7 32	8 32			9 33		16 1		1057	11 45	1227			1251	2 15		3 14	1 3		4 44
16 Quaker's Yard (H.L.) **F** arr.			7 35	8 35			9 36		10 4		11 0	11 48	1230			1254	2 18	W	3 18	1 3		4 47
Mls Quaker's Yard (H.L.) dp.				8 43					10 7		11 3					1257		2 30		3 27	4	
— 2¼ Aberfan				8 49					1013		11 9					1 3		2 36		3 33	4 1?	
— 5¼ Abercanaid									1026		1120					1 15		2 46		3 43	4 22	
— 7 Merthyr 484 ..... arr.				3 55	9 3		1005		1031		1125	10	1 09			1 20		2 56		3 52	4 30	5 14
Quaker's Yard (H.L.) .. dep.				7 38	8 38		9 42				11 51	1238					2 19	Stop	3 21			4 53
17¾ Penrhiwceiber (H.L.) 90 ..				7 43	8 43		9 47				11 56	1238					2 24		3 26			4 53 aft
19 Mountain Ash (Cardiff Rd.)				7 48	8 47		9 55				12 0	1244	m				2 29		3 30			4 57
21¾ Cwmbach Halt				7 53							1127		1230			1 10						5 5
22½ Aberdare (H.L.) ¶ { arr.				7 57	8 55		10 3				1131	12 8	1254			1 14		3 38			5	5 9
26¾ Hirwaun 92 { dep.		7 18		8 0	8 58		1010	10 40				12 16				1 27		3 40			5	5 9
— 92 Merthyr ..... dep.		7 26		8 11	9 6		1018	10 48				12 16				1 38		3 44				5 24
— 92 Merthyr ..... dep.		7 N 0			8 N40 mrn		9 48	10 30			1 N55					1 5		3 20				4 52
Hirwaun ¶ ..... dep.		7 28		8 12	9 8	m	1021	11 6	m			12 27				1 39		3 51				5 25
32½ Glyn Neath		7 41		8 29	9 20		1036	11 22				12 41				1 58		4 10				5 43
35½ Resolven ¶		7 47		8 36	9 26	9 57	1043	11 30			1145	12 48				3 5		4 19				5 50
40 Aberdylais		7 56		8 49	9 35	1010	1053	11 40			1158	12 57				2 23		3 38	4 19			6 6
Neath (Riverside)		mrn		8 55		1016						12 3				2 29		3 43				6 9
Neath Abbey ¶				9 0		1020					12 7					2 33		3 47				6 13
Briton Ferry Road ..		6 54		9 10		1027					121 4					2 43		3 54				6 23
48½ Swansea (E. D., 75 .. ar.		7 1		9 17		1034					1220					2 50		4 1				6 30
41¾ **Neath** (General) **67**. 87a.		8 4		9 43			11 1				1 5							4 27				
43½ Skewen		8 10		9 49			11 7	11 54			1 12							4 33				
46 Llansamlet		8 16		9 55			12 0				1 18							4 39				
48¾ Landore **62**. 75		8 22		10 1			1119	12 6			1 25							4 45				
9¾ Swansea (High St.) 491 arr.		8 27		10 6			1124	12 11			1 30							4 50				

PONTYPOOL ROAD, CARDIFF, MERTHYR, NEATH, and SWANSEA.

Week Days—Continued.

Down.																	Suns.		
123 London (Pad.) ..... dep.	aft	aft	aft	aft	aft	aft				3 55	m	m		4 V30	5 55	5 55		A 1255	1245
123 Bristol (T.M.) ,,		2735		4 12		5 20		6 5 5		6 27	7 20	7 20		7 20	7 20		A 1255	5 40
123 Newport (High St.) ,,		4 42		5 20		6 27	7 42	742			8 35		9 35		7 40	6 7
Pontypool Road ..... dep.	4 50	5 2		6 20		7 42	8 5	8		8 109	35		8 20	6 90
Pontypool **A** 78	4 55	5 6		6 36		7 47	8 9	8 10		8 20		9 14	9 40		8 25	6 96
Hafodyrynys Plat. (i below)	5 11		m	6 64		7 57		8 20		m	9 50		8 40	7 13
Crumlin (H.L.) ¶ **B** 81	5 11	Stop		6 64 41		8 6	8 2	8 32		10 0	10 3		8 47	7 25
Pentwynmawr Platform ..	5 15			6 6 45		8 6		8 37		10 0		10 9		8 51	7 31
Penmaen Halt				6 11				8 37			1014		8 56	
Oakdale Halt ..... arr.				6 23				8 43			1023		9 5	
Pontllanfraith **C** 505	5 18			6 48			8 15			1017	11		8 467	20
Hengoed (High Level) **D**	5 24			6 55			8 22			1017 11	17		8 55	7 26
Nelson & Llancaiach 129 ar.	5 31 aft						8 22			1024	11		9 2	7 32
Cardiff (Queen St.) ¶ dep.		4 55					7 30 8 30	8 50		9 22		9822	1022		8 56	6 45
Llanishen ¶		5 7					7 42 8 50			9 35		9935	10 39		9 8	6 57
Caerphilly		5 16		5 28			7 53 8 59		9 35		9842	1039		9 17	7 6
Llanbradach				3 35			8 0 8 79 13		9 42		9849	1046		9 24	7 13
Ystrad Mynach ..... [129		Stop		5 42			8 6 9 18		9 49 52				Stop	9 31	7 20
Nelson & Llancaiach				5 47			9 553 9 53		9 57					9 8	
129 Dowlais **H** ..... arr.		6 27					10 32						1212	
Nelson & Llancaiach ..... dep.	5 32			5 49		7 12	8 23 9 20			9 58	1032		1131 9	27 33
Treharris	5 36			5 53		7 16	8 27 9 24			10 5	1037		1135 9	37 37
Quaker's Yard (H.L.) **F** 92 ar.	m 5 39			5 56		7 19	8 30 9 27			10 5	1039 11 15		1138 9	40 44
Quaker's Yard (H.L.) dep.	5 42			6 6		9 30					1141		9 45	
Aberfan	5 41			6 6		9 36			1016		1147		9 51	
Abercanaid	5 51			6 6		9 46			1026		1157		10 1	
Merthyr 484 ..... arr.	5 58			6 27		9 14 9 53			1033		C 1116		12 4 9 37 10	8
Quaker's Yard (H.L.) .. dep.	5 42		Stop		7 22		8 33				1040 11 16		Stop	9 27 7	45
Penrhiwceiber (H.L.) 90 ..	5 47			6 10 aft		7 27	8 38				1045 11 21		9 17 51	
Mountain Ash (Cardiff Rd.)	5 52	m		6 32		m 8 16 8 42				1049 11 25		9 22 7 56	
Cwmbach Halt			6 10 aft									9 27	
Aberdare (H.L.) ¶ { arr.	6 0		6 14 m		7 40	8 148 248	50		1057 11 33			9 30 8	4
{ dep.	6 6		6 20		Stop 7 58	8 52						9 34 8	14
Hirwaun 92	6 14		6 30	Stop	9 0					aft	9 42 8	23
92 Merthyr ..... dep.		5 N45			7 N30		8 N30					8 50 7 30	
Hirwaun ¶ ..... dep.	6 17		6 31		8 0	9 16				m	9 46 8	26
Glyn Neath	6 31		6 50		8 15	9 16				1045	10 0 8	39
Resolven ¶	6 37		6 57		8 21	9 28				1051	10 6 8	45
Aberdylais	6 46		7 6		8 30	9 41				11 4	
Neath (Riverside)		aft		aft aft	aft						S	
Neath Abbey ¶										ngt.	
Briton Ferry Road 78 ..			aft	aft aft	aft						
Swansea (E. Dk.) 76 arr.						9 39				11 8 1247 1023 9	0
Neath (General) **67**. 87a.	6 50 6 59		7 14 7 46 8 0 8 34 8 45		9 39				11 8 1247 1023 9	0
Skewen	7 5		8 6 8 31	9 45						
Llansamlet	7 11		8 12 8 37	9 51						
Landore **62**. 76	7 17		8 18 8 43	9 57				1 0	
Swansea (High St.) 491 arr.	7 22		8 28 23	9 8	10 2			5 1045 9 20	

A Clarence Street; about ¼ mile to Crane Street Station. —
A Saturday night.
B About ¼ mile to Low Level Station. **B** Via Hengoed.
C About ¼ mile to L. M. & S. Station.
O Passengers change from High Level to Low Level at Quaker's Yard.
D Adjoining Hengoed (L.L.) Station and about ¼ mile to Maesycwmmer Station.
D Arrives Hengoed (H.L.) at 813 mrn. and 4 20 aft. respectively.
E Except Saturdays.
F Adjoins Low Level Station.
F By Road Motor to Aberdare (H.L.) Station.
G Arrives Ystrad Mynach at 8 24 mrn. **H** Cae Harris.
J Passengers can depart Stapleton Road at 7 32 aft.
K Mondays only.
m or **N** Rail Motor Car, one class only.
S or **S** Saturdays only.
X Departs London (Paddington) at 9 25 aft. on Sundays.
V Via Bristol.
W Workmen's Train.
X Arrives at 2 55 aft.
Y Departs at 1 55 aft. on Sats.
Z Departs at 2 45 aft. on Sats.
¶ "Halts" at Treowen, between Crumlin (High Level) and Pentwynmawr Platform; at Heath (High Level), between Cardiff and Llanishen; at Cefn On, between Llanishen and Caerphilly; at Troedyrhiw, between Aberfan and Abercanaid; at Trecynon, between Aberdare and Hirwaun; at Rhigos and at Pontwalby, between Hirwaun and Glyn Neath; at Meiyncourt and at Clyne, between Resolven and Aberdylais; and at Cardonnel, between Neath Abbey and Briton Ferry Road.

PONTYPOOL ROAD

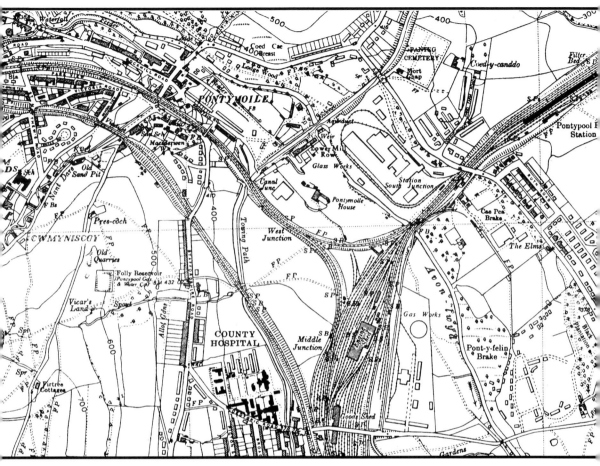

III.   Our route crosses the top of this 1953 map, which is at 6ins to 1 mile. Below it on the left
is the Monmouthshire Eastern Valleys Line between Blaenavon and Newport; it carried passenger
trains until 1962. Clarence Street station is top left and Pontypool Road top right.

1. The station was named Pontypool Newport Road until May 1854 and was south of the road bridge until 1st March 1908. Its up loop platform is on the extreme left. The house was retained for use by the station master after the new station was completed. (British Railways)

February 1942

PONTYPOOL ROAD, CARDIFF, MERTHYR, NEATH, and SWANSEA.

Week Days only.

Miles from Pontypool Rd	Down.	mrn	mrn	mrn	mrn	mrn	mrn	mrn	mrn	mrn	mrn	mrn	mrn	aft	aft S	mrn Ⓑ	mrn	aft	Ⓑ E	aft	aft E		aft	aft	aft	aft	aft E	aft	aft S	aft S	aft E
125	London (Pad.) ......dep.	..	..	..	..	1255	..	..	..	..	..	..	5 30	..	..	..	9 15	..	9 15	..	..	..	..	..	..	1 55	..	..	..	..	..
125	Bristol (T.M.) 64.. "	..	..	..	..	5 50	..	..	..	..	..	..	9 5	..	..	9 5	12 37	..	12U57	..	..	..	..	..	..	4 40	..	5 0	..	..	..
125	Newport .... "	..	Ⓑ	..	..	7 16	..	Ⓑ	..	..	7 55	..	10 6	..	..	1040	1 13	..	2 25	..	..	..	..	..	..	5 35	..	6 49	..	..	..
—	Pontypool Road ......dep.	Workmen's Train.	6 42	..	..	7 45	..	8 16	..	..	8 40	..	11 0	..	..	1 15	2 28	..	4 4	..	..	..	..	..	..	6 20	..	7 38	..	..	..
1¾	Pontypool A 80		6 46	..	..	7 50	..	8 20	..	..	8 45	..	11 5	..	..	1 19	2 33	..	4 9	..	..	..	..	..	..	6 25	..	7 43	..	..	..
5¼	Hafodyrynys Platform.....		6 56	..	..	8 0	..	8 30	..	..	8 57	..	11 15	..	..	1 29	2 42	..	4 19	..	..	..	..	..	..	6 34	..	7 53	..	..	..
6¾	Crumlin (H. Level) ¶ 81...		7 0	..	..	8 5	..	8 34	..	..	9 1	..	11 20	..	..	1 33	2 47	..	4 25	..	..	..	..	..	..	6 39	..	7 58	..	..	..
7¾	Pentwynmawr Platform...		7 4	..	..	8 9	..	8 40	..	..	9 5	..	11 24	..	..	1 37	2 50	..	4 31	..	..	..	..	..	..	6 42	..	8 2	..	..	..
9½	Penmaen Halt.......arr.		..	..	..	..	..	..	..	..	..	..	..	..	..	..	..	..	..	..	..	..	..	..	..	..	..	..	..	..	..
9	Pontllanfraith C 565......	..	7 9	..	..	8 12	..	8 43	..	..	9 7	..	11 27	..	..	1 40	2 53	..	4 34	..	..	..	..	..	..	6 45	..	8 5	..	..	..
11	Hengoed (High Level) D...	6 17	7 14	..	..	8 17	..	8 47	..	..	9 12	..	11 36	..	..	1 45	3 0	..	4 40	..	..	..	..	..	..	6 49	..	8 16	..	..	..
14	Nelson & Llancaiach 89 ar.	6 23	7 20	..	..	8 23	..	..	..	..	9 18	Ⓑ	11 42	..	..	1 50	3 5	Ⓑ	4 46	..	..	..	..	..	..	6 55	..	8 22	Ⓑ	..	..
—	Mls Cardiff (Queen St) ¶dp.	5H15	..	6 40	..	..	..	Except Saturdays and School Holidays.	8 18	..	..	1010	10H58	..	..	..	2 H 0	3 18	3H45	..	4 38	..	..	5 0	..	5H30	..	7H30	8 35	..	..
—	3¼ Llanishen ¶...........	5H24	..	6 49	..	..	..		8 27	..	..	1019	11 H7	..	..	..	2 H9	3 27	3H54	..	4 47	..	..	5 9	Ⓑ	5H41	..	7H39	8 44	..	..
—	7 Caerphilly.............	5H37	..	7 2	..	..	..		8 37	..	..	1030	11H17	..	..	..	2H20	3 38	4 H3	..	4 58	..	..	5 18	5 26	5H52	..	7H50	8 55	..	..
—	9¾ Llanbradach	5H44	..	7 10	Ⓑ	..	..		8 43	..	..	1036	11H23	..	..	..	2H26	3 44	4H18	..	5 5	..	Ⓑ	..	5 32	5H59	..	7H57	9 1	..	..
—	12¼ Ystrad Mynach.....[89	5H53	..	7 18	7 20	..	..		8 50	8 55	..	1043	11H29	..	1215	..	2H32	3 51	4H24	..	5 11	..	5 15	..	5 39	6 H6	..	8 H3	9 9	..	..
—	14¼ Nelson & Llancaiach ar	..	..	..	7 26	..	..		..	9 0	..	1046	..	..	1219	..	..	3 56	..	..	..	..	5 21	..	5 43	..	..	..	9 14	..	..
—	Nelson & Llancaiach ¶ dep.	..	..	..	7 28	8 24	..		..	..	9 19	1048	11 43	..	1220	1 51	3 6	3 59	4 47	Except Saturdays and School Holidays.	..	..	5 22	..	5 44	6 56	..	8 23	9 15	..	..
15¼	Treharris ....[84	..	..	..	7 34	8 30	..		..	..	9 25	1053	11 49	..	1225	1 56	3 11	4 5	4 53		..	..	5 27	..	5 49	7 1	..	8 29	9 20	..	..
16	Quaker's Yard (H.L.) F arr.	..	..	..	7 36	8 32	Ⓑ		..	..	9 27	1055	11 51	Ⓑ	1227	1 58	3 13	4 7	4 55		..	..	5 30	..	5 51	7 2	Ⓑ	8 31	9 22	..	..
—	Mls Quaker's Yd. (H.L) ¶dp	..	..	..	..	..	8 40		..	..	..	11 0	..	1210	..	..	..	4 8	..		..	..	..	..	5 52	..	7 15	..	9 23	..	..
—	2¼ Aberfan ¶.............	..	..	..	..	..	8 47		..	..	..	11 7	..	1218	..	..	..	4 15	..		..	..	..	..	5 59	..	7 22	..	9 30	..	..
—	5¼ Abercanaid............	..	..	..	..	..	8 56		..	..	..	1116	..	1226	..	..	..	4 23	..		..	..	..	..	6 8	..	7 31	..	9 39	..	..
—	7 Merthyr 486......arr.	..	..	..	..	..	9 1		..	..	..	1121	..	1232	..	..	..	4 29	..		..	..	..	..	6 13	..	7 36	..	9 44	..	..
—	Quaker's Yard (H.L.)..dep.	..	..	..	7 37	8 35	..	..	..	..	9 30	..	11 54	..	1228	2 2	3 16	..	4 58		..	..	5 33	..	..	7 3	..	8 34	..	..	..
17¼	Penrhiwceiber (H.L.) 89...	..	..	..	7 41	8 40	..	..	..	..	9 34	..	11 59	..	1232	2 7	3 21	..	5 3		..	..	5 38	..	..	7 8	..	8 39	..	..	..
19	Mountain Ash (Cardiff Rd.)	..	..	..	7 45	8 44	..	..	..	..	9 38	..	12 3	..	1236	2 10	3 24	..	5 7		..	..	5 42	..	..	7 12	..	8 43	..	..	..
21¼	Cwmbach Halt...........	..	..	..	7 49	..	..	..	..	..	9 42	..	12 7	..	1240	2 14	3 31	..	5 11		..	..	..	..	..	7 17	..	..	..	..	..
22¾	Aberdare (H.L.) ¶... arr.	..	..	..	7 53	8 52	..	..	..	..	9 46	..	12 12	..	1245	2 18	3 34	..	5 15		..	..	5 51	..	..	7 21	..	8 51	..	..	..
	Aberdare (H.L.) dep.	..	..	..	7 59	..	..	..	..	..	9 47	..	12 15	..	..	2 20	3 38	..	..		..	..	..	..	..	7 33	..	..	..	..	..
26½	Hirwaun 96 ....arr.	..	..	..	8 9	..	..	..	..	..	9 58	..	12 23	..	..	2 32	3 50	..	..	Ⓑ	..	..	..	..	..	7 41	..	..	..	..	..
—	96 Merthyr..........dep.	..	..	..	7 45	..	..	..	..	..	9T30	..	11T53	..	..	2 0	3T19	..	..	4 49	..	..	..	..	..	7T15	..	..	..	..	..
—	Hirwaun ¶............dep.	..	..	..	8 10	..	..	..	..	..	10 0	..	12 25	..	..	2 33	3 54	..	..	5 10	..	..	..	..	..	7 47	..	..	..	..	..
32¼	Glyn Neath..............	..	..	..	8 34	..	..	..	..	..	1014	..	12 39	..	..	2 51	4 8	..	..	5 28	..	..	..	..	..	8 1	..	..	..	1020	1115
35½	Resolven ¶..............	..	..	..	8 40	..	..	..	..	..	1020	..	12 45	..	..	2 58	4 14	..	..	..	..	..	..	..	..	8 7	..	..	..	1025	1122
40	Aberdylais..............	..	..	..	8 51	..	..	..	..	..	1033	..	12 53	..	..	3 10	4 23	..	..	..	..	..	..	..	..	8 15	..	..	..	1034	1137
41¾	Neath (Gen) 64, 69, 89 arr.	..	..	..	8L55	..	..	..	..	..	1037	..	12 57	..	..	3 15	4 27	..	..	..	..	..	..	..	..	8 20	..	..	..	1040	1141
49½	64 Swansea (High St.) arr.	..	..	..	9 36	..	..	..	..	..	11 8	..	1 39	..	..	3 51	4 54	..	..	..	..	..	..	..	..	9 10	..	..	..	4a31	4a31

A Clarence Street, about ¼ mile to Crane Street Station. *a* Mrn. **C** About ¼ mile to L. M. & S. Sta. **D** Adjoining Hengoed (L. L.) Station and about ¼ mile to Maesycwmmer Station. **E** or E Except Saturdays. **F** Adjoins Low Level Station. H Via Hengoed. L Neath (Riverside Sta.). **S** or S Sats only. T Third class only. U Stapleton Road. ¶ For "Halts," see page 94. Ⓑ Third class only.

2.   The new spacious station had two long through platforms in island configuration, with bays between them at each end. This is the south end and the coaches are at the platform commonly used by Neath trains. (M.J.Stretton coll.)

3.   The platform lines were flanked by running lines connected by scissors crossovers near their mid-points. Class 5600 0-6-2T no. 6636 is on the down one on 27th May 1956 and on the left is the main building which was demolished in November 1963. It was linked to the platforms by a subway. (F.Hornby)

4.   A northward panorama on 12th October 1957 features 2-8-0 no. 3824 running in with coal empties. The up main line is between the signals; up and down goods lines are on the left. In the distance is the 65-lever Pontypool Station North box, which lasted until 4th November 1973. (D.Johnson coll.)

Great Western Railway.
QUAKERS' YARD TO
BIRMINGHAM [SNOW HILL
Via Tenbury and Cradley
THIRD CLASS
Issued subject to the conditions stated
on the Co's. Time Bills.   (WL)
Birmingham S.H. Birmingham S.H

040

906

Gt Western Ry   Gt Western Ry
PENRHIWCEIBER   PENRHIWCEIBER
High Level   High Level
TO
PONTYPOOL RD
THIRD   CLASS
2/3   Fare   2/3
Issued subject to the conditions & regulations set
out in the Company's Time Tables Bills & Notices
Pontypool Rd   Pontypool Rd

906

5.　　Turning round, we see the carriage sidings between the up main and down goods lines, with an 0-6-0PT on one of them. A van train stands in the Monmouth bay (No. 4). Service to that town ceased in May 1955. (Lens of Sutton coll.)

6.　　Moving to the other side of the vans, we complete our survey by looking at the two down lines and the mid-platform signals. These were controlled by one of two back-to-back 13-lever frames in Station Middle box. There were 17 signalmen on the payroll for many years.
(Lens of Sutton coll.)

7.   A view from the road bridge on 26th
March 1959 has the station in the background
and 4300 class 2-6-0 no. 7325 departing with
the 2.25pm to Neath. This is the only tender
engine on a Neath train in this volume.
(S.Rickard/J & J coll.)

8.   The south end is seen on 5th May 1962,
with the bay platform (No. 3) for Neath trains,
centre. Its signal has a route indicator below it.
On the right are the ends of the sidings seen in
picture 6. (Nelson coll./T.Walsh)

9.   An overview from the approach road on 27th June 1963 includes a van train held at signals
on the down main, while other vans are about to be loaded with parcels for the Vale of Neath line.
Station Middle box projects through the roof; it became a ground frame in October 1957 and closed
on 9th October 1967, when the crossovers were taken out of use. (P.J.Garland/R.S.Carpenter)

10.   Staff cars stand on the site of the original station on 18th August 1962, as 0-6-0PT no. 7724 waits in front of Pontypool Road Station South box. Its outline is in the centre arch in picture 8. Its 163-lever frame was not used after 8th October 1979.(M.Dart)

The subsequent name changes and views of the dramatic decline of the station can be found in our *Hereford to Newport* album.

11.   No. 5029 *Nunney Castle* waits to depart south on 20th August 1963, having been relegated to freight work. It survived and was often to be found at the Didcot Railway Centre. (B.S.Jennings)

12.   Turning round, we find 0-6-2T no. 5647 with the 1.10pm for Neath at platform 1. It started out with five coaches, but dropped two at Aberdare High Level. (B.S.Jennings)

SOUTH OF
PONTYPOOL ROAD

13.   The engine shed was south of the triangular junction, see map III. This view is from an ex-GWR railcar working the 8.30am Pontypool Road to Newport service on 27th May 1956. The ramp on the right leads to the coal stage, which is under the pitched roof. (F.Hornby)

14.   The wagons on the right are on the level track beyond the coal stage. Recorded on 30th June 1957 was no. 40091, an ex-LMS 2-6-2T of a type introduced in 1935. (M.Dart)

15.   The BR shed was coded 86G and this is its south end on 13th July 1958. It was completed in stages in 1869-79, the larger part being a roundhouse. Nearest is no. 8444, one of the 9400 class 0-6-0PTs introduced in 1947. (H.C.Casserley)

16.   A view north from Coedygric Road Viaduct (visible in the left background of picture 13) on 26th March 1959 features the massive running shed. The lines to the goods shed are on the left and the running lines are on the extreme right, beyond the signals. (S.Rickard/J & J coll.)

17.   Part of the turntable at the centre of the roundhouse is visible in this photograph, the first of three from 18th August 1962. Hiding in the inevitable gloom are nos 8495 and 5775. (M.Dart)

18.   No. 8781 was station pilot that day and is attached to an ex-GWR shunters truck. The gasworks was east of the engine shed and is described in caption 20. There were usually about 90 locomotives allocated to the shed. (M.Dart)

19.   Bent rail ends are evident near the ash pit and the roof was much patched. On one of the eight roads is 4-6-0 no. 46129 *The Scottish Horse*. The shed closed in May 1965. (M.Dart)

20.   The new Panteg gasworks was opened in March 1949; the previous one is shown top left on map III and top right on the one opposite. The private siding passes through a gateway, top left, and came into use in May 1947 for the conveyance of construction materials. Between 73,000 and 100,000 tons of coal were delivered annually. Extra plant was added in 1963, but this used oil. A Fowler 0-4-0 diesel was provided initially and a similar Hibberd arrived in 1960. Both were new. Coal ceased to be used in March 1967 and demolition took place in 1973. (Wales Gas Board)

PONTYPOOL CLARENCE STREET

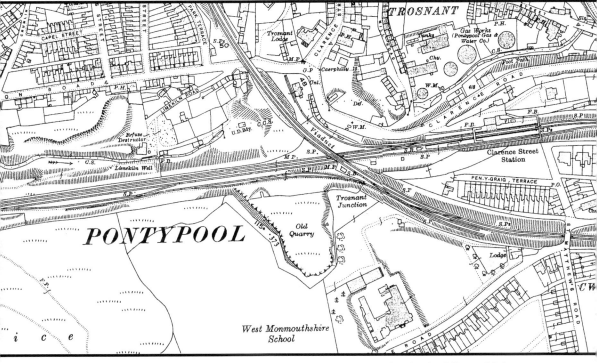

IV.   The 1921 survey has the station on the right and includes the single siding, which was part of a goods yard until 3rd April 1911. It served a timber yard until 1927. The Eastern Valleys Line curves across the map. A loading dock and a short siding is shown above the PON of PONTYPOOL. This had earlier been the site of Clarence Wagon Shops. At the west end of the down platform is an 18-lever signal box. Its work was taken over by Trosnant Junction box on 22nd February 1933, after it had been raised three feet to improve visibility.

21.   A westward view has the Eastern Valleys bridge in the distance. The station was simply "Pontypool" until 1867 and then had the suffix "Town" until 1881, when it was changed to "Clarence Street". A staff of 17 in 1923 was reduced to six over ten years.
(Stephenson Locomotive Society coll.)

22.   A 1957 eastward view from the up platform includes a public footbridge. Beyond it, there was a loop on the down side in the 1920s for Pantymoel Coal Yard. Most traces of the first five miles of the route have been lost under road improvements. (Stations UK)

23.   A panorama from the public footbridge, also in 1957, has on the left "Third Line". This was a reversible goods line which ran between Middle Junction (see bottom of map III) and Old Furnace Colliery, a distance of over two miles. There was no connection at West Junction. It was little used after 1934 and became a siding in 1949. (Stations UK)

Pontypool (Clarence Street)	1903	1913	1923	1933
Passenger tickets issued	100567	112538	234686	152246
Season tickets issued	*	*	393	189
Parcels forwarded	19985	20523	3660	3351
General goods forwarded (tons)	819	closed for goods		
Coal and coke received (tons)	10	traffic 1911		
Other minerals received (tons)	45			
General goods received (tons)	3952			
Trucks of livestock handled	-			
(* not available.)				

24.   This bridge carries the Eastern Valley route over the Vale of Neath line, the connection between the two being on the right. The back of Trosnant Junction box is visible; it closed on 15th November 1968. There is no evidence of Third Line in this 1963 photo, due to embankment widening work in 1959 when a new connecting link was provided. It was singled in 1968.
(P.J.Garland/R.S.Carpenter)

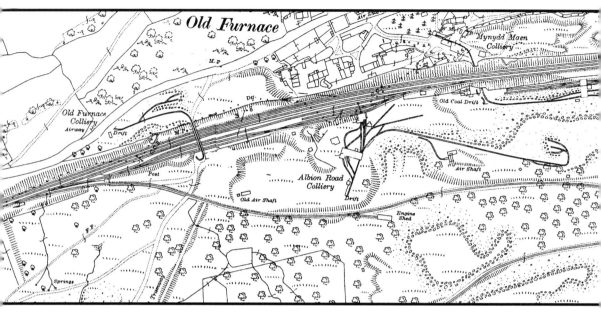

V.   Third Line runs across this map and the previous one, terminating off the left of this extract which is from 1921 and includes three collieries their outputs all going over Third Line. This also served Gwent Wagon Shops. After reversal beyond the right border, trains could use the line at the bottom to reach Upper Race Brickworks, Glyn Collieries (Race Colliery), Glyn Quarry, Glyn Tillery Colliery, Blaendare Brickworks, Blaendare Ironworks, Blaendare Slope Colliery and Cwm Lickey Colliery.

HAFODYRYNYS COLLIERY

VI.   Further tracks were laid down north of the running lines after this map was produced in 1921. Two signal boxes were provided.

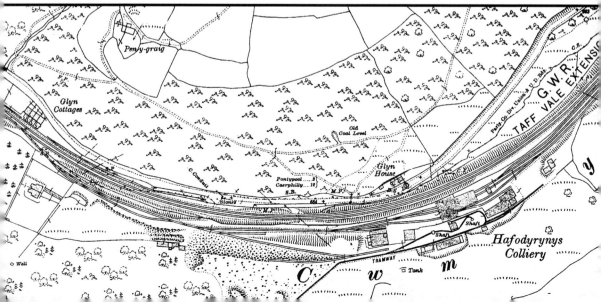

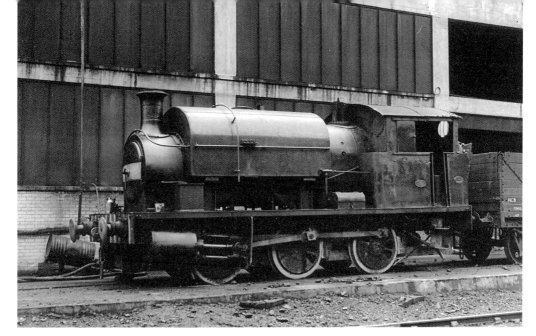

25.   An undated photograph features Manning Wardle no. 1942, which was built in 1918. (R.Holmes)

26.   Shunting on 4th April 1969 was Hunslet 0-6-0ST *Glendower*, which was new in 1954, works no. 3810. (M.Dart)

27.   Standing with other more historic items on 21st May 1973 was another Austerity Hunslet, no. 3817. The last coal was raised early in 1979 and the last train left (for Aberthaw Power Station) on 1st April. The single line from here to Pontypool Road ran via Trosnant Junction and was officially closed on 9th April 1979. (T.Heavyside)

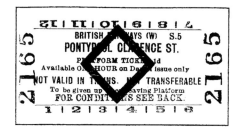

CRUMLIN VALLEYS
COLLIERS PLATFORM

28.   The colliery sidings came into use in 1911; to the east was Blaendare Sidings signal box, while to the west was Cefn Crib box, until 1958. An eastbound train passes the platform, which was not used after 6th November 1961. (R.Holmes)

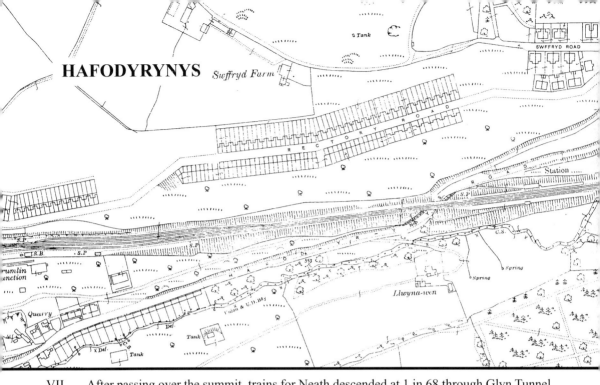

HAFODYRYNYS Swffryd Farm

VII.   After passing over the summit, trains for Neath descended at 1 in 68 through Glyn Tunnel (280yds) to reach the station (right) on this 1921 map. On the left is Crumlin Junction, where a single track branched north to Llanhilleth.

29.   The platforms came into use on 1st May 1913 and are seen in about 1936. The Ebbw Valley spreads out in the distance. (Stations UK)

30.   Glyn Tunnel is in the distance in this eastward view from July 1958. The station had been unstaffed since 8th August 1932 and was fenced off. (R.M.Casserley)

31.   The smoke drifts around as 0-6-2T no. 6652 brakes hard on the 1 in 65 descent on 26th September 1960. The train is the 1.05pm Pontypool Road to Neath. The diamond indicates the presence of track circuiting. (H.C.Casserley)

32.   Crumlin Junction is seen with two ringed arms for the goods lines. On the left are the passenger lines, those curving left soon converged to a single line (after 22nd April 1928) to cross Crumlin Viaduct. There had been a temporary station in this vicinity from 20th August 1855 to 15th October 1857. The line to the right opened on 3rd September 1855 and descended at 1 in 42 to Llanhilleth Junction and carried coal from the Upper Ebbw Valley to the Midlands via Pontypool Road. It also carried workmens trains between Brynmawr and Glascoed, on the line to Monmouth, at one period. (GWR Magazine)

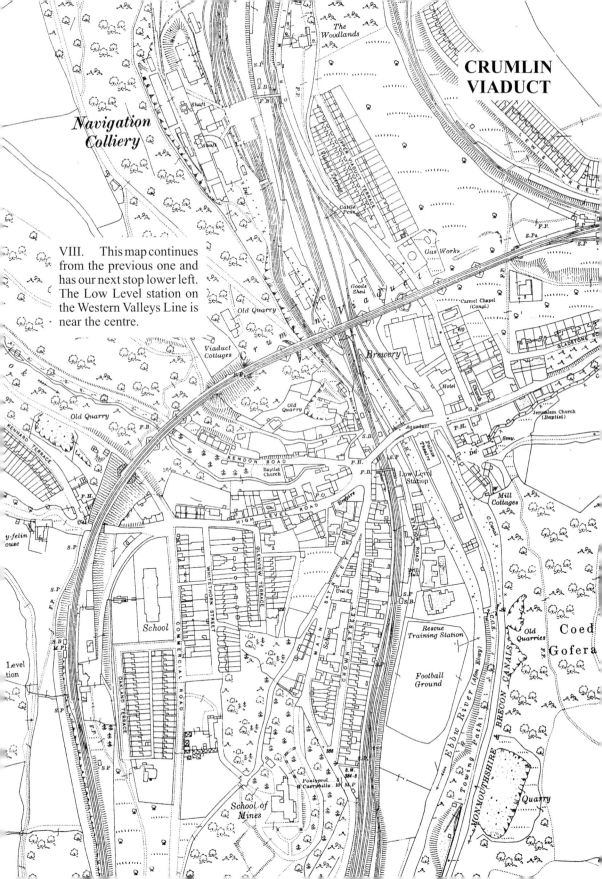

CRUMLIN VIADUCT

Navigation Colliery

VIII.   This map continues from the previous one and has our next stop lower left. The Low Level station on the Western Valleys Line is near the centre.

33.   The line crossed the Ebbw Valley on seven spans and the adjacent Kendon Valley on a further three. The large building (lower centre) was a brewery and had earlier been Crumlin Iron Works. The viaduct took four years to build and opened on 1st June 1857. (Lens of Sutton coll.)

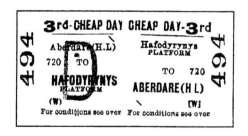

34.   Another postcard view includes the boiler house and engine house of Navigation Colliery, which produced steam coal for ships. The maximum height of the structure was 208ft and the total length (including abutments) was 1658ft. (P.Q.Treloar coll.)

35.   Descending onto the structure on 27th July 1963 is the 1.10pm from Pontypool Road. All trains were subject to an 8mph speed limit. The main components were tubular cast iron columns, 16ft in length and 12ins external diameter. A total of 1196 tons of castings came from Falkirk and 880 tons of wrought iron was produced in Blaenavon. The iron deck plates were replaced by steel in 1928. (P.J.Garland/R.S.Carpenter)

36. Another 1963 photograph shows the spectacular view from a train on the viaduct, this featuring the Low Level station which had closed to passengers on 30th April 1962. Demolition of the viaduct took place in April 1967, but a disused single line to Ebbw Vale Steelworks was still in place on the floor of the valley in 2005. Restoration of the line for passenger services began that year. (B.S.Jennings)

37. The highest piers were 30 x 60ft at the base and 15 x 30ft at the top. All the spans were 150ft in length and each consisted of four pin-jointed, rivetted wrought-iron truss girders. No. 6627 is heading and no. 6634 is banking on 27th May 1963. The four abutments have been listed Grade II and this pair are railed as viewing platforms. (W.Potter/R.M.Casserley coll.)

38. The headland separating the two parts of the viaduct is seen from the curved path leading up to the High Level station. It is 28th March 1964 and no. 6640 heads the 11.0am Aberdare to Pontypool Road train. (T.J.Edgington)

CRUMLIN HIGH LEVEL

39.   This view towards the viaduct includes the signal box, which was in use until line closure. The staff numbered 23 in 1923, but were down to 17 by 1935. Some of these worked at nearby sidings and at Crumlin Junction. (Lens of Sutton coll.)

Crumlin (High Level)	1903	1913	1923	1933
Passenger tickets issued	81121	118811	96131	20135
Season tickets issued	*	*	115	86
Parcels forwarded	2394	3513	2082	805
General goods forwarded (tons)	13	168	86	95
Coal and coke received (tons)	103	3556	-	25
Other minerals received (tons)	31	6524	2777	422
General goods received (tons)	39	1840	10125	11782
Trucks of livestock handled	-	-	-	-
(* not available.)				

40.   The view towards Neath in about 1936 includes another glimpse of the up platform shelter. The reverse curves necessitated the offsetting of the signals from their tracks. Only the station masters house remains standing. (Stations UK)

41.   The rear of the train is on the single line on the viaduct as 0-6-2T no. 6675 is about to enter the down platform. The valley marked the end of the first part of the Taff Vale Extension of the NAHR. (M.J.Stretton coll.)

42.   The then obligatory fire buckets are hanging on the wall of the toilet block for gentlemen. As customary, this was largely devoid of a roof. (E.Wilmshurst)

43.   Many of the features discussed are seen more clearly in this March 1964 view of 0-6-0PT no. 9488 waiting for the single line over the viaduct to be clear. The inclined lamp shade was to aid token exchange. The footbridge was erected around 1930 and additional steps gave direct access to a footpath above the station, where the notice board is situated. (T.J.Edgington)

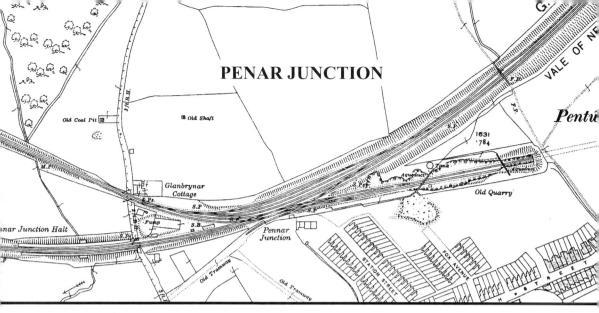

PENAR JUNCTION

IX.   Our journey takes us from top right to lower left; the line top right is from Markham Colliery and the line entering the tunnel is to Halls Road Junction, on the Western Valleys line. The section south of Penar Junction was closed between 20th November 1967 and 2nd May 1970, when the Vale of Neath route was reopened westward, as a single line to Bird-in-Hand Junction. This 1921 map shows the arrangement existing from about 1900 to 1944, when the running lines were singled north of the signal box.

44.   A 1963 shot from a Neath-bound train shows the single connection to Markham Colliery. Halls Tramroad had been on this alignment and through Penar Tunnel. It had crossed the TVE of the NAHR on the level here. The section northwards was converted to standard gauge by the GWR on 10th March 1886. Railcars ran over part of it between 1927 and 1939. Four weekday trips from Crumlin High Level to Oakdale Halt were worked initially, but this was reduced to one, Fridays only, as far as Penmaen Halt, the other stop on the branch, in 1932. (P.J.Garland/R.S.Carpenter)

45.   No. D6990 is hauling a train of empties out of Penar Tunnel (239yds) on 9th November 1967. The signals on the left faced a loop used for reversal. (M.Dart)

46.   This is the west end of the signal box, on the same day. It had a 61-lever frame and closed on 20th November 1967, when the sidings beyond it were also taken out of use. (M.Dart)

47.   Also visible in the previous photo are the remains of Penar Junction Halt, which was open from 1st January 1913 to 1st January 1917. It served much longer as a watering place for up trains, as seen here in 1958. (D.Lawrence)

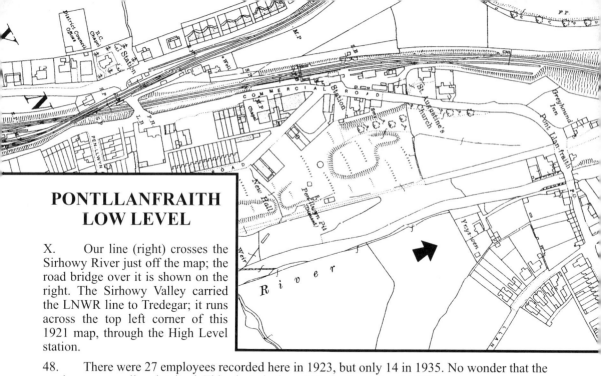

PONTLLANFRAITH LOW LEVEL

X.   Our line (right) crosses the Sirhowy River just off the map; the road bridge over it is shown on the right. The Sirhowy Valley carried the LNWR line to Tredegar; it runs across the top left corner of this 1921 map, through the High Level station.

48.   There were 27 employees recorded here in 1923, but only 14 in 1935. No wonder that the gardens were well maintained. This photo is thought to be from about 1910. (R.S.Carpenter coll.)

49.   The station was named Tredegar Junction until 1st May 1905, when it became Pontllanfraith. "Low Level" was added on 19th July 1950, although it is not shown in this picture from April 1955. The footbridge was erected in 1913. (H.C.Casserley)

50.   An excursion to Porthcawl on 14th July 1957 required two 0-6-0PTs, nos 3683 and 3703. Barry and Penarth were the only other places of any size nearby with worthwhile beaches. The site is now occupied by the A4048 dual carriageway. (T.J.Edgington)

51.   A Royal Mail van waits to receive bags off the next down train on 10th July 1958. There is clear evidence of the platform having been lengthened at a greater height. (R.M.Casserley)

Pontllanfraith	1903	1913	1923	1933
Passenger tickets issued	39263	84358	63866	20383
Season tickets issued	*	*	224	246
Parcels forwarded	2802	5814	15215	27512
General goods forwarded (tons)	133	2242	390	72
Coal and coke received (tons)	261	1317	1822	563
Other minerals received (tons)	2942	5185	2632	1721
General goods received (tons)	1580	5820	6873	5899
Trucks of livestock handled	55	250	114	11

(* not available.)

52. The meaning of HANCOO in picture 49 now becomes apparent, as 0-6-2T no. 5658 approaches on 23rd October 1959. The 16-lever signal box closed with the line. (R.S.Carpenter)

53. The architectural details are similar to those seen in picture no. 1. The goods yard is evident; this closed on 4th May 1964, only a few weeks before the line itself. The photo is from July 1963. (P.J.Garland/R.S.Carpenter)

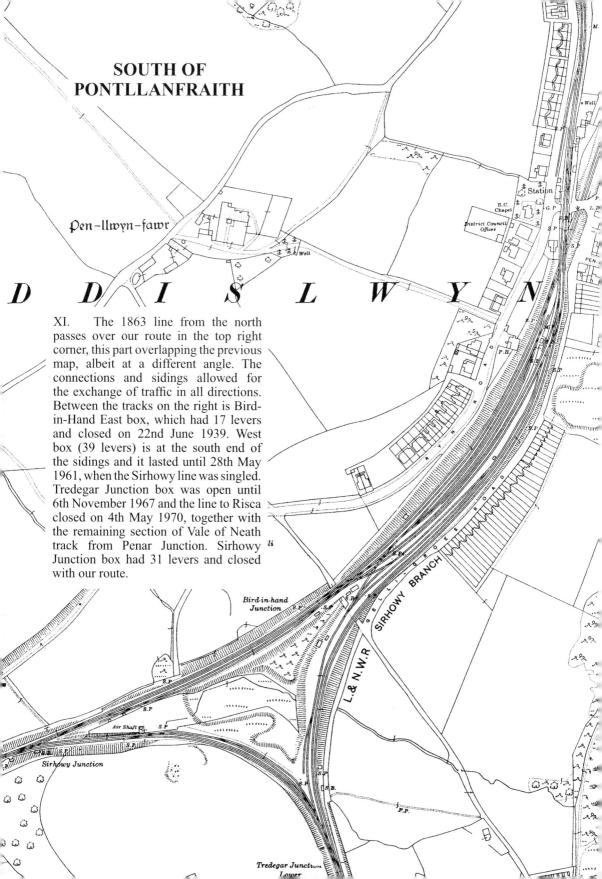

SOUTH OF PONTLLANFRAITH

Pen-llwyn-fawr

D   D   I   S   L   W   Y   N

XI.   The 1863 line from the north passes over our route in the top right corner, this part overlapping the previous map, albeit at a different angle. The connections and sidings allowed for the exchange of traffic in all directions. Between the tracks on the right is Bird-in-Hand East box, which had 17 levers and closed on 22nd June 1939. West box (39 levers) is at the south end of the sidings and it lasted until 28th May 1961, when the Sirhowy line was singled. Tredegar Junction box was open until 6th November 1967 and the line to Risca closed on 4th May 1970, together with the remaining section of Vale of Neath track from Penar Junction. Sirhowy Junction box had 31 levers and closed with our route.

Station

R.C. Chapel

District Council Offices

Bird-in-hand Junction

SIRHOWY BRANCH

L. & N.W.R

Air Shaft

Sirhowy Junction

Tredegar Junction Lower

54. A southward panorama across Bird-in-Hand Junction in August 1962 has Tredegar Junction box in the distance. Gelligroes Colliery had sidings within the triangle, on the north and southwest sides - see map. (M.Dart)

55. We are looking eastward towards the exchange sidings beyond Bird-in-Hand box on 27th July 1963. The name came from a nearby public house. The area is now occupied by houses. (P.J.Garland/R.S.Carpenter)

56. Bryn Tunnel was 398yds in length and was cut through the high ground between the Sirhowy and the Rhymney Valleys. The summit was near its mid-point. This is the east portal in 1962. (M.Dart)

EAST OF HENGOED

57.   Maesycwmmer Junction is on the right of the next map and the connection to the Brecon &
Merthyr route curves away on the right in this view from the road bridge on 23rd February 1956.
No. 9712 is working the 11.15am from Aberdare and is passing the signal box, which had 31 levers
and closed on 15th June 1964, with the lines over the viaduct. The routes in the other directions
were in use until 20th November 1967. The only regular passenger service northwards had been
for Glascoed munition workers. (S.Rickard/J & J coll.)

2nd - HALF-DAY EXCURSION	HALF-DAY - 2nd EXCURSION
Neath General to	Pontllanfraith to
PONTLLAN-FRAITH L.L. via Aberdare	NEATH GENERAL via Aberdare
(W) For conditions see over	(W) For conditions see over

58.   After passing over the junction, down trains ran onto Hengoed Viaduct and travelled over the Rhymney River, then the boundary between England and Wales. The 2.25pm from Pontypool Road is leaving the structure on 13th May 1961, behind 2-6-2T no. 4169. (R.E.Toop)

59.   The viaduct was 299yds in length and was recorded trackless on 31st March 1972. It was still standing unused more than 30 years later. The 16 arches reach a maximum height of 130ft. (M.Dart)

HENGOED
HIGH LEVEL

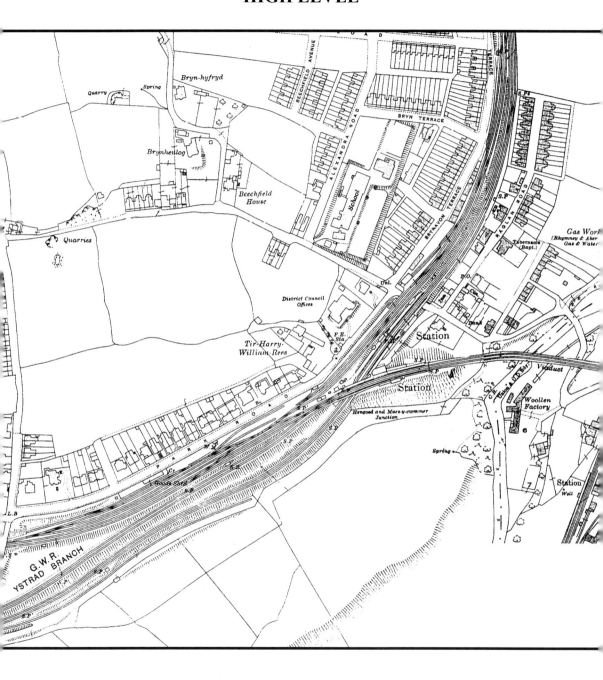

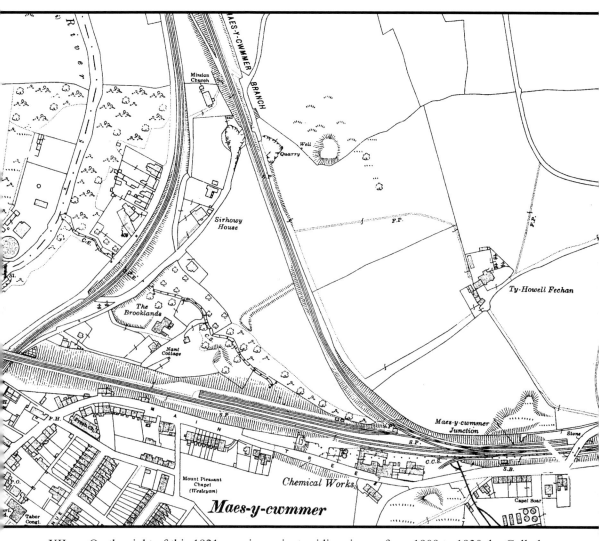

XII. On the right of this 1921 map is a private siding, in use from 1909 to 1930, by Gellydeg Brickworks. The Maesycwmmer Tar & Chemical Works had one until 1954. The other sidings were for exchange traffic. On the right of the left page is part of the B&MR station, which can be seen in pictures 90-92 in our *Brecon to Newport* album. That line closed at the end of 1962.

60. Seen near the goods yard is the signal box, which had 39 levers. The Ystrad branch is on the left in this view from about 1920. (GWR Magazine)

61. An April 1955 panorama shows the relationship between the viaduct, the High Level platforms and the former Rhymney Railway tracks, which are still in use to that town. A scheme was successfully launched in 2004 to create a cycleway on the viaduct. (H.C.Casserley)

62.   A 1958 westward view shows the raised platform extensions, which pass over the spans featured in the previous photograph. The train is on the goods connection to the Rhymney line. Traffic was light in the 1950s, but in 1923 a staff of 38 had been needed here. It was over 23 throughout the 1930s. (H.C.Casserley)

63.   A wider angle from almost the same viewpoint reveals the full nameboard and also the brick screen, behind which gentlemen were ordered to complete the adjustment of their clothes. (Stations UK)

64.	Seen from above the Rhymney line on 4th October 1958 is 0-6-0PT no. 6431 destined for Neath. Some trains were scheduled to wait here ten minutes for connections with that line. A short path linked the stations and there was a common booking office. (G.Adams/M.J.Stretton coll.)

65.   Barely visible against the field beyond the goods yard is the yard crane. Local freight traffic ceased on 13th July 1964. No. 6115 is working the 11.25am from Neath on 13th May 1961. (R.E.Toop)

66.   This is the southern end of the connection provided by the RR for coal traffic. It bypasses the Low Level station and was closed on 15th July 1964. The High Level up platform end is on the right in this picture from 1962. (M.Dart)

67. Curving in the foreground are the other connections to the former RR, these running south towards Ystrad Mynach. They were used by excursions and workmens trains at various times and were closed on 6th May 1963. The photo is from July 1963. (P.J.Garland/R.S.Carpenter)

A journey of 2 hrs 12 mins was on offer to workers in June 1955.

Hengoed (High Levels)	1903	1913	1923	1933
Passenger tickets issued	54996	83602	61279	20103
Season tickets issued	*	*	360	98
Parcels forwarded	1472	1983	1994	1896
General goods forwarded (tons)	786	1008	460	-
Coal and coke received (tons)	1922	2339	585	-
Other minerals received (tons)	1861	3298	4451	-
General goods received (tons)	1121	3489	2853	-
Trucks of livestock handled	2	-	-	-

(* not available.)

Miles from Pontypool Rd.			am
	164 **London** (Pad.) ..	dep	..
	164 Bristol (T.M.)	"	....
	164 Newport	"	..
	Pontypool Road ...	dep	Workmen's Train
1¼	Pontypool **A**	..	
5½	Hafodyrynys Platform		
6¼	Crumlin (High Level) **B** ..		
7	Treowen Halt		
7¾	Pentwynmawr Platform ..		
9	Pontllanfraith (L.L.) **H** ..		
11	Hengoed (H.L.) **D** ..	arr	
—	Mls **Cardiff** (Q. St.) ..	dep	5 15
—	12½ Ystrad Mynach		5 48
—	13½ Hengoed (L.L.) **F.**	arr	5 52
—	Hengoed (H.L.).. ..	dep	6 17
14	**Nelson and Llancaiach**	arr	6 23
		dep	6 47
14¾	Trelewis Halt		To Dowlais (Cae Harris), arr 7 27 am (Table 139)
15¼	Treharris		
16	**Quaker's Yd.** (H.L.) **G**	arr	
22¾	125 Merthyr ¶	arr	
—	**Quaker's Yd.** (H.L.).	dep	
17¾	Penrhiwceiber (H.L.) ..		
19	Mountain Ash (Cardiff Rd.)		
21¼	Cwmbach Halt		
22¾	**Aberdare** (H.L.) ..	arr	
		dep	
23¾	Trecynon Halt		
26¼	Hirwaun	arr	

68.   Our final pictures are from 5th October 1963, when the 3.50pm Aberdare High Level to Pontypool Road was hauled by 0-6-2T no. 6661. Originally called "Rhymney Junction", the name became "Hengoed & Maesycwmmer" on 1st July 1906 and finally "Hengoed High Level" on 1st July 1924. (E.Wilmshurst)

69.   The 3.55pm from Pontypool Road to Neath was in the charge of 0-6-2T no. 5659. There was no footbridge and so passengers used this crossing. No buildings remain. (E.Wilmshurst)

WEST OF HENGOED

70.   We now have two indifferent, but interesting, winter views from the road shown lower left on the map. They are both from 23rd February 1956 and this includes the viaduct, 2-8-0 no. 2870 and the signal box, which closed on 15th June 1964. (S.Rickard/J & J coll.)

71.   Moving to the right, the photographer recorded 0-6-0PT no. 4626 with a down freight on the Rhymney line, with the Neath line on the left. (S.Rickard/J & J coll.)

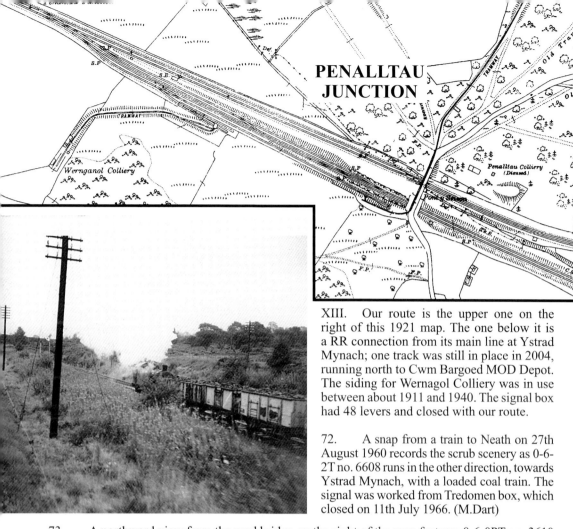

PENALLTAU JUNCTION

XIII. Our route is the upper one on the right of this 1921 map. The one below it is a RR connection from its main line at Ystrad Mynach; one track was still in place in 2004, running north to Cwm Bargoed MOD Depot. The siding for Wernagol Colliery was in use between about 1911 and 1940. The signal box had 48 levers and closed with our route.

72. A snap from a train to Neath on 27th August 1960 records the scrub scenery as 0-6-2T no. 6608 runs in the other direction, towards Ystrad Mynach, with a loaded coal train. The signal was worked from Tredomen box, which closed on 11th July 1966. (M.Dart)

73. A northward view from the road bridge on the right of the map features 0-6-0PT no. 3610 with the 11.15am from Aberdare on 27th April 1957. On the left is the line to Ystrad Mynach and the down loop. (S.Rickard/J & J coll.)

EAST OF NELSON & LLANCAIACH

74.   No. 37227 was recorded with a spoil train on 25th September 1980. The sidings were on both sides of the line and were known variously as Ash Pile, Shale Disposal and Bog East. At least one siding was in use from 1977. (D.H.Mitchell)

75.   The commencement of the Pontypridd branch was recorded from a passing train in August 1962. A short length was retained to serve two sidings, which are shown on the next map. (M.Dart)

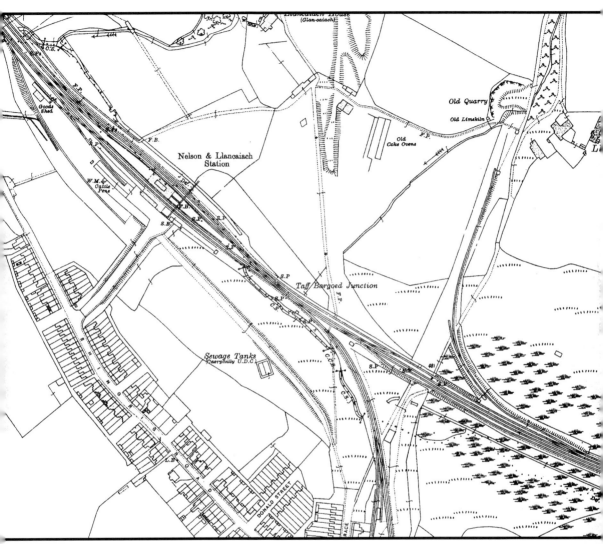

XIV.   On the right of this 1921 map is our route flanked by a down refuge siding and an up goods loop, from which trails the disused Llancaiach Colliery siding. At the bottom is the Taff Vale Railway from Pontypridd, which closed in the 1930s. Top left, the lines to Dowlais Cae Harris are the upper pair, Neath trains using the lower pair. The platforms were east of Taff Bargoed Junction until 1912, but there were none for TVR trains. This company had a single platform, further south, called "Nelson".

76.   A westward postcard view shows the first station in about 1908. It had no canopies or footbridge; there was just one fire. At almost 500ft above sea level, some weather protection was really required. The route eastward often carried over 50 trains each way daily around 1913. The signal box is to the left of the loco and near the junction. (Lens of Sutton coll.)

Nelson and Llancafach	1903	1913	1923	1933
Passenger tickets issued	59356	83883	68712	20346
Season tickets issued	*	*	189	111
Parcels forwarded	5701	9372	5754	8288
General goods forwarded (tons)	116	395	214	62
Coal and coke received (tons)	373	1225	300	34
Other minerals received (tons)	1003	921	1550	607
General goods received (tons)	1390	2597	1914	4252
Trucks of livestock handled	76	43	90	67

(* not available.)

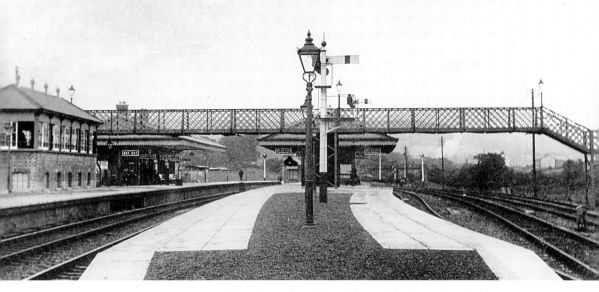

77.	The footbridge was extended to the right to link with a public footpath. The signal box had 94 levers when closed on 18th September 1968. It was termed "West" in 1912-32; "East" was ½ mile to the east until that time. (Lens of Sutton coll.)

78.	The 3.15pm departure for Dowlais Cae Harris was recorded from the road bridge on 20th September 1954. It was hauled by 0-6-2T no. 5660. There had been 22 employees here in 1923, the figure dropping to 15 by 1932. (D.Kelk/R.M.Casserley coll.)

79.   Two trains appear to be at the outer face of the island platform. It was usually used by the Dowlais services, some of which ran to and from Ystrad Mynach, via Penalltau Junction. (Lens of Sutton coll.)

(top right)
80.   The 3.50pm Aberdare to Pontypool Road was headed by 0-6-0PT no. 9711 on 2nd March 1963. Little had altered here in the previous 50 years, except the signals. (E.Wilmshurst)

(right)
81.   The pairs of starting signals at the east end were for the main line and the up loop, which was more than ½ mile in length. It had been signalled for passenger trains since at least 1920. The connection on the right leads to the lines seen in picture 75.
(P.J.Garland/R.S.Carpenter)

82.	The signalling at the west end was simpler, as Dowlais trains only left from this platform. However, goods trains could depart in response to the ringed signal on the right. Both pictures are from 1963. (P.J.Garland/R.S.Carpenter)

83.	The 11.05am from Neath arrived behind 2-6-2T no. 4157 on 28th March 1964. Nelson West ground frame is in the distance. (T.J.Edgington)

84.   The 12.49 (Saturdays only) to Dowlais (Cae Harris) was recorded on 11th April 1964, behind 0-6-2T no. 5677. Passenger services were withdrawn on 15th June of that year. (R.E.Toop)

85.   No. 6643 worked the "Rambling 56" on 31st July 1965. The Swansea Railway Club ran from Cardiff via Radyr, Penrhos Junction, Aber Junction, Ystrad Mynach, Dowlais (return), Bargoed, Pengam and Risca to Newport High Street. The track had been realigned for freight traffic. (R.E.Toop)

86.   No. 37248 heads east with a load of coal from Trelewis Colliery on 25th September 1980. The siding on the left was lifted in 1981; those on the right served Nelson Coal Depot until 2nd November 1981, but remained in place. (D.H.Mitchell)

87.   "The Rod Mill Rattler" stopped at the same point as the train in picture 83 on 23rd October 1982. The Monmouthshire Railway Society started at Newport and visited Rod Mill (Cardiff), Trelewis, Dowlais (return), Caerphilly and Coryton. (D.H.Mitchell)

TRELEWIS HALT

XV.   Treharris station is at the bottom of the left page of this 1921 map and the goods yard is to the left of that. It had a 30cwt crane and closed on 7th October 1963. The extensive Taff Merthyr Colliery was established immediately to the east of Ocean Deep Navigation and its sidings were laid down in 1927-28. The connection trailed off the up line and can be seen in picture 91. On the left of this page is Treharris box (14 levers) although it had closed in 1904. Trelewis halt was opened on 9th July 1934, when the population was about 3000. It was situated immediately north of the bridge carrying the line over Glyn Bargoed Road, right.

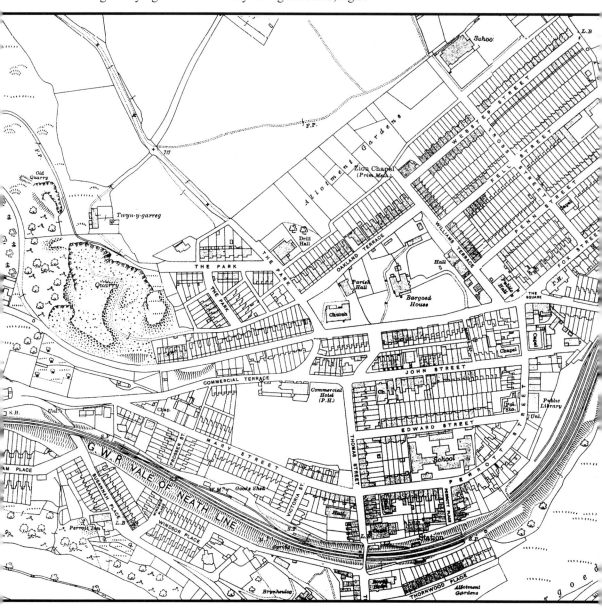

88.   This eastward panorama is from the cutting which spans the two pages of the map. Trelewis is in the background and Treharris is behind us. On the left is Ocean Navigation box which had 21 levers and closed on 24th July 1927. (R.Marrows coll.)

89.   The 6.02pm from Neath is approaching in gloomy weather on 15th July 1959 and is headed by 2-6-2T no. 5102. Special inclined lights were provided for the foot crossing. (R.M.Casserley)

90.   A 1963 view in the other direction includes the small porch on the ticket office. An iron hut was provided as shelter on the down platform. (E.Wilmshurst)

91.   The 1927 colliery connection is in the foreground of this 1964 photograph from Bontnewydd Terrace. Centre is Ocean & Taff Merthyr box, which was in use between those years. It had 39 levers. (R.Marrows)

92.   This view shows the close proximity of the headgears of Ocean Deep Navigation and Taff Merthyr Collieries. The sidings of the two were connected together in 1978 to form a triangle with the main line. This had been closed completely west of Treharris in 1964. Coal traffic east thereof ceased in March 1996. No. 37798 is seen in this southward panorama on 21st October 1991. (R.Marrows)

TREHARRIS

93.   The station opened on 2nd June 1890, the booking office being at road level. The crowd on the bridge maybe witnessing the arrival of the first steam railmotor. (Lens of Sutton coll.)

94.   A down train was the subject of a postcard in the 1920s; the locomotive appears to be a Metro tank. The valley is deeply incised and sharply curved in this area. It is reported that passenger trains were not allowed to pass on this curve. (Lens of Sutton coll.)

QUAKERS YARD HIGH LEVEL

95.   This eastward view is from June 1922, at a time when there was a staff of 30, a figure that still applied in 1935. "Yard" refers to a burial ground, about one mile to the south. There was little habitation near the junction initially. (M.J.Stretton coll.)

96.   A picture from about 1930 shows the west end of the platforms and that the north end of the footbridge ended at street level in Edwardsville. This development took place in around 1900 and Mr Edwards was chairman of the committee involved. (Stations UK)

VALE RAILWAY

Quarry

South Wales & Monmouthshire Truant School

XVI.   Our route runs from right to left and passes over the single line viaduct into the 703yd long Quakers Yard Tunnel (just off the map) to reach the Cynon Valley. Still in use is the Merthyr to Cardiff line (top to bottom) of the TVR. It made its first connection with another standard gauge line via the curve on the right. The three viaducts shown are over the River Taff. The line on the one top left was built jointly by the GWR and RR and was opened in 1886. It ran to Merthyr via Aberfan and closed in 1951, due to subsidence. The Low Level station opened in 1858 and High Level followed in 1864. The NA&HR originally had its own platform, near those of the TVR. The 1919 map is at 22ins to 1mile.

Viaduct

S.P.

S.P.

S.P.

S.P.

S.P.

S.P.

S.P.

S.B.

M.P.

S.P.

S.P.

S.P.

S.P.

S.B.

TY N Y-BANWAN ROAD

TREHARNE RD.

EDWARDSVILLE

Station
(High Level)

P.H   L.B.

S.P.

S.B.

Quaker's Yard Junction

Station
(Low Level)

S.B.

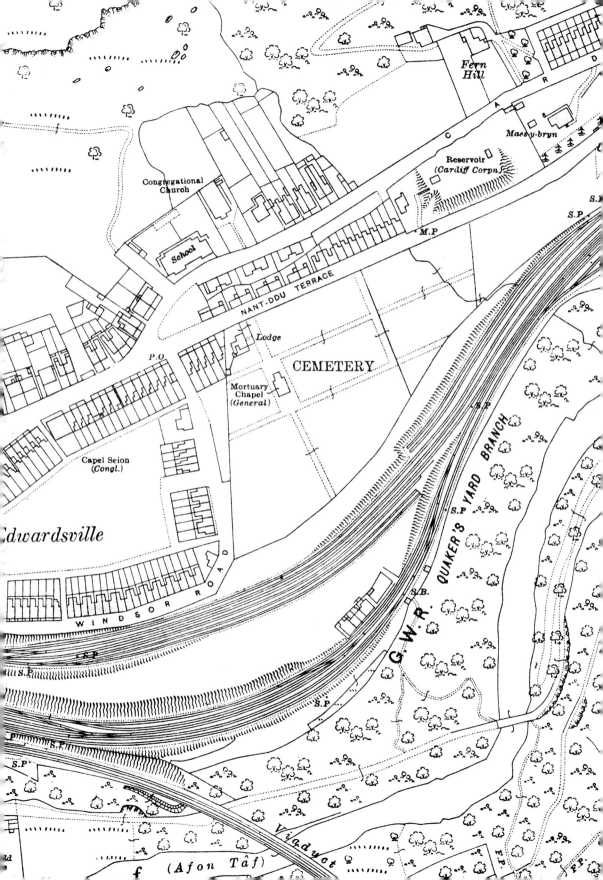

Fern Hill

Maes-y-bryn

Reservoir
(Cardiff Corpn)

Congregational
Church

School

R A C

M.P

S.P

S.P

S.P

NANT-DDU TERRACE

Lodge

CEMETERY

P.O

Mortuary
Chapel
(General)

S.P

Capel Seion
(Congl.)

S.P

Edwardsville

S.B.

G.W.R.

QUAKER'S YARD BRANCH

WINDSOR ROAD

S&P

S.P

S.P

S.P

S.P

F.P.

Viaduct

F.P.

(Afon Tâf)

97.　　The 1.05pm Pontypool Road to Neath was hauled by 0-6-2T no. 6649 on 11th April 1955, when it stopped by the terraced gardens. It is coupled to an autocoach. (R.M.Casserley)

→

98.　　Students of sanitary engineering will be pleased to see this otherwise hidden cast iron urinal. There were a number on the GWR, but they were far from common. (R.M.Casserley)

→

99.　　No. 6628 was working from Neath on 13th August 1957 when it was recorded approaching the crossing seen in the previous picture. The suffix "High Level" was used from the 1890s. (B.K.B.Green/M.Dart coll.)

100.   Seen on the same day is 0-6-0PT ————→
no. 8444 with the two down sidings in the
background. Traffic declined in the 1950s, but
increased following diversion of freight from
the Abergavenny to Merthyr route.
(B.K.B.Green/M.Dart coll.)

101.   Two porters stand near the bottom of the
steps as the 12.36 to Pontypool Road emerges
from valley mist on 30th November 1957, headed
by 0-6-2T no. 5659. The photographer joined
the train to take the next view. (R.M.Casserley)

————→

102.   Quakers Yard East Junction box is in the distance (in line with the telegraph pole). It had
19 levers, was in use from 1904 to 15th June 1964 and is where the steep incline on the right joins
our route. The location is on the right of the map. (R.M.Casserley)

103.   It is 4th October 1958 and no. 6431 is taking on Taff water to complete its journey to Neath. The pump house is shown on the map, near the left border.
(G.Davis/M.J.Stretton coll.)

104.   A   westward   panorama   from   the footbridge on 6th March 1958 features 0-6-0PT no. 6410 with the 11.15am Aberdare High Level to Pontypool Road. Note the severe speed restriction over the viaduct.
(S.Rickard/J & J coll.)

105.   A few minutes later, the photographer was able to record the same train, plus the bridge between the platforms of the Low Level station. The stunning scenery appears in both pictures.
(S.Rickard/J & J coll.)

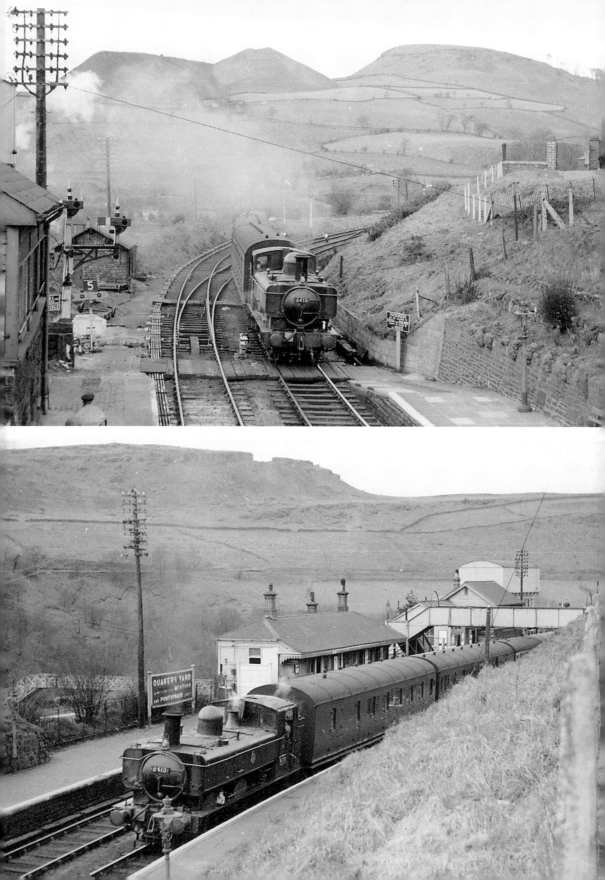

106.   The water tank is centre, beyond the signal box. Our route to Mountain Ash passes through the high ground in the background by way of Quakers Yard Tunnel. This junction was paradise for the rural railway lover. (H.C.Casserley)

107.   Smart new signs arrived not long before closure, but 2-6-2T no. 4174 has lost its number plate. However, no one wanted the original sign's posts. The photo is undated. The single line through the tunnel was a tokenless section and very unpleasant owing to its small dimensions. (D.Lawrence)

108.   Our final view of this charming location is from 5th October 1963. The 3.35pm from Aberdare is behind 0-6-2T no. 6661. All has been lost, but the surroundings are as splendid as ever. Only the Low Level down platform remains in use. (E.Wilmshurst)

WEST OF QUAKERS YARD

109.	The line to Neath is on the left in this shot from a train on 18th August 1962. The double track to Merthyr had lost its passenger service on 12th February 1951, due to the unsafe nature of the Taff Viaduct, but a short length was retained for shunting purposes. (M.Dart)

110.	We look north along the Taff Valley, the alignment being up the left border of map XVI. Both viaducts had been braced with timber in about 1918, owing to mining subsidence. The Brecon Beacons are in the distance. The line on the left soon entered the tunnel and on emerging it became double track, near Quakers Yard West Tunnel box. It had 17 levers and closed with the route. There was an up refuge siding nearby. The Glamorganshire Canal had passed over the tunnel, near its east portal. Both viaducts were demolished in 1969. The Penydaren Tramway had passed under the right arch of the nearest viaduct. Its gauge was 4ft 4ins and carried the world's first steam locomotive in 1804, which was built by Trevithick. (J.Langford coll.)

PENRHIWCEIBER HIGH LEVEL

XVII.   The route descended steeply through Quakers Yard Tunnel and along its first mile in the Cynon Valley, to come onto this 1921 map lower right. The station is shown above the first road bridge. Between it and the river are Powell Duffryn's private lines, which linked its Cwmcynon Colliery with exchange sidings on the route of the TVR, one mile to the south, until 1975.

111.	This postcard panorama contains typical terraced houses for miners and has the station on our route in the foreground. The TVR station is on the right; the map shows that the two are separated by the river. Note that the booking office is close to the road. (Lens of Sutton coll.)

112.	An eastbound freight was recorded on 15th July 1959, with 2-6-2T no. 4255 in charge. Cwmcynon Colliery winding gear is in the background; the pit opened in 1878. This station came into use on 15th June 1899 and became "High Level" on 1st July 1924. (H.C.Casserley)

113. The entire structure was built of timber to minimise weight on the embankment on which it was constructed. This is the 2.10pm from Pontypool Road on 22nd June 1963 and is hauled by 0-6-2T no. 6628. (E.Wilmshurst)

114. After closure in 1964, part of the former Vale of Neath route was used by the National Coal Board, west of the colliery, from 1968 to 1981. Hunslet 0-6-0ST no. 8 is running from Penrhiwceiber to Mountain Ash on 17th April 1978. (M.Dart)

MOUNTAIN ASH (CARDIFF ROAD)

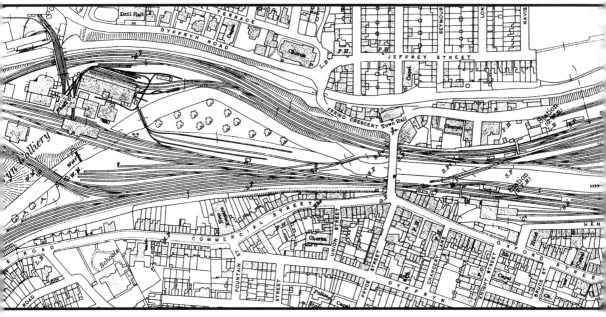

XVIII. The upper two tracks on the right of this 1921 map form our route, those below them being colliery lines from Cwm Cynon, which continue through Navigation Colliery and on to Duffryn

115. This panorama is from the road bridge on the left page and includes the GWR station, together with Navigation Colliery, supplier of steam coal to countless ships. The line to the TVR over the river was disconnected in March 1913. (Lens of Sutton coll.)

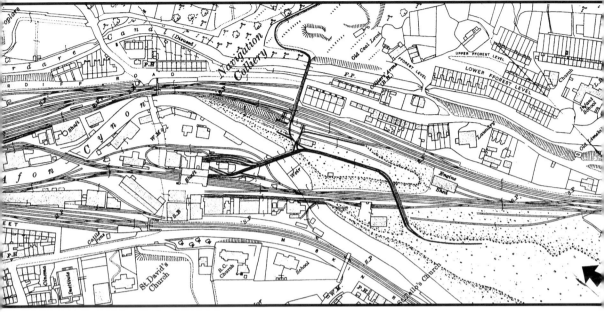

Colliery. On the lower part of the map is the TVR route, which lost its passenger service in 1964, but had it restored in 1988.

116. The suffix was added to the name on 1st July 1924; the running-in board was photographed in about 1958, from a train from Neath. (Lens of Sutton coll.)

117.   The photographer has his back to the goods shed in 1958 to record the connection from the down line to the yard. There had been 30-40 employees here in the 1930s. The down platform was built as an island in 1868, when the route was doubled. (H.C.Casserley)

118.   A mixed freight runs up the valley behind 2-8-0 class 8F no. 48525, a type introduced by the LMS in 1935. The viewpoint is as for picture 115, but the mountains are clearer. There were 12 coal trains a day each way back in 1913. The footbridge was added in 1904. (D.Lawrence)

119.   Cresselley Crossing is near the road bridge over the river on the right page. Note that the gates do not swing over the third track and that its footbridge is of a different pattern. Cresselley Crossing box had 16 levers and closed with the route. The photo is from 1963, as is the next one. (P.J.Garland/R.S.Carpenter)

120.   Mountain Ash box also closed with the route, but had 30 levers. Our final view contains all the characteristics of the line: interesting signals, stations of character and superb scenery. (E.Wilmshurst)

MP Middleton Press
EVOLVING THE ULTIMATE RAIL ENCYCLOPEDIA

Easebourne Lane, Midhurst, West Sussex.
GU29 9AZ   Tel:01730 813169
www.middletonpress.co.uk email:info@middletonpress.co.uk
A-0 906520 B-1 873793 C-1 901706 D-1 904474

OOP Out of Print at time of printing - Please check current availability **BROCHURE AVAILABLE SHOWING NEW TITLES**